PR
*What G.*

Hendrix is a new voice in the lineage of Southern writers who have made art of both their homeplace's beauties and horrors. Yet she does anything but follow that line straight; her vigorous and vibrant language runs and bucks into the spaces between woman and man, love and hate, and near and far, where the scent of jasmine and blood hang together in the air. Hendrix's poems are like the splinter of glass she describes driven into a heel—they'll stay with you. But, rather than pain, the reader of this book experiences the sharpness of bold ideas, the shimmer of sultry imagery, and intimacies it's a kind of earthly blessing to share.

—ROSE MCLARNEY, author of *Colorfast* (Penguin, 2024), *Forage* (Penguin, 2019), *Its Day Being Gone* (National Poetry Series winner, Penguin, 2015), and *The Always Broken Plates of Mountains* (Four Way Books, 2012)

*What Good is Heaven* offers an extended meditation on mercy, and a tribute—courageous and stunning—to the people and places that raise us. Utterly transporting, drenched in both the dazzling and the disastrous, this remarkable debut conjures an atmospheric and personal South that is deeply queer and kindred, full of animals, hymnals, and heat. In Hendrix's capable hands, one is pulled forward, rapt, through many dangers. I fell into the world of these poems with my senses awakened, heart beating fast. This book, and the survival at its heart, will become a part of you.

—GABRIELLE BATES, author of *Judas Goat* (Tin House, 2023)

Country wisdom informed by authentic, idiosyncratic experiences with family and the natural world, instead of cornpone stereotypes and unreasonable natural history I see in most contemporary "Southern" writing, anchors Raye Hendrix's *What Good is Heaven*. Hendrix knows a shellcracker from a warmouth and a bluegill. She's pulled on the teat of a cow who recently had a stillborn calf and felt that cow's instinct to bend her neck to see what was feeding from her. She's stalked the hen-house bandits and respects the scavengers who clean up the dead. And through these explorations of the natural world, she evokes human pursuits and anxieties concerning religion and identity and lineage and inheritances that are always present as subtle substrata in the poems. Or, perhaps, she's tricked me into believing that she acquired this acumen firsthand because she's listened so closely to the dirt farmers' and old salts' and pea-shellers' stories and accepts the woods and fields and lakes as mentors and foxes the foxes and coyotes the coyotes. Either way, I'm fully enthralled by Hendrix's pinch of the world and her wanderings through it. Hell, she seems like kin.

—ADAM VINES, author of *Lures* (LSU Press, 2022), *Out of Speech* (LSU Press, 2018), and *The Coal Life* (University of Arkansas Press, 2012)

"An astonishing, knock-out collection of poems. This is what I want most in a book—visceral poems that are acutely alive and wrestling with the world and ourselves. These poems tackle the violence of the Deep South, which is the violence of America, and do not look away. Raye Hendrix writes like a boxer fights—with courage, grit, grace, tenderness, and an unforgettable urgency. This is why we come to poetry in the first place: to feel something, to be changed."

—ANSEL ELKINS, author of *Blue Yodel* (Yale Series of Younger Poets winner, 2015)

"Raye Hendrix is an honest poet—her verse is not 'on the pulse,' it is the pulse. In her stunning debut, *What Good is Heaven*, Hendrix writes the brutal beauty of the Alabama wilds and the humans' wildness in it. In poems that are fresh, surprising, revelatory and ferociously open, Hendrix chronicles the bloody slaughter that is family, religion, identity and love—a soup of secrets in the hot, strange South. Hendrix shows the reader the heart of prey while simultaneously reminding us that 'everything must eat.' It is a remarkable collection."

—ASHLEY M. JONES, Alabama Poet Laureate (2022-2026) and author of *REPARATIONS NOW!* (Hub City Press, 2021), *dark // thing* (Pleiades Press, 2018), and *Magic City Gospel* (Hub City Press, 2017)

"*What Good is Heaven* is a collection heavy with blood and labor: 'slow curve / of a mother's spine : riverbank / solid enough to stand.' Raye Hendrix is a poet lighting the daily violence of the deeply gendered South. The interior Hendrix reveals to us is a geography without bystanders, and through complex lyric tenderness we must ask the same questions as the poems' speaker: 'Is it wrong of me to want / this to survive? To die?' In *What Good is Heaven* there is a place for all our contradictions of being. The speaker in Hendrix's poems has found a life in dismantling those contradictions that diminish and limit us—making music in their place."

—C.T. SALAZAR, author of *Headless John the Baptist Hitchhiking* (Acre Books, 2022)

# WHAT GOOD IS HEAVEN

# WHAT GOOD IS HEAVEN

## Poems

## RAYE HENDRIX

The TRP Southern Poetry Breakthrough Series:
Alabama

TRP: THE UNIVERSITY PRESS OF SHSU
HUNTSVILLE, TEXAS 77341

Library of Congress Cataloging-in-Publication Data
Names: Hendrix, Raye, author.
Title: What good is heaven : poems / Raye Hendrix.
Other titles: TRP Southern poetry breakthrough series.
Description: First edition. | Huntsville : TRP: The University Press of
    SHSU, [2024] | Series: TRP Southern poetry breakthrough series: Alabama
Identifiers: LCCN 2024008716 (print) | LCCN 2024008717 (ebook) | ISBN
    9781680033717 (paperback) | ISBN 9781680033724 (ebook)
Subjects: LCSH: Rural sexual minorities—Alabama—Poetry. | Farm
    life—Alabama—Poetry. | Coming of age—Alabama—Poetry. | Gender
    identity—Poetry. | LCGFT: Poetry. | Queer poetry.
Classification: LCC PS3608.E5436 W47 2024 (print) | LCC PS3608.E5436
    (ebook) | DDC 811/.6—dc23/eng/20240301
LC record available at https://lccn.loc.gov/2024008716
LC ebook record available at https://lccn.loc.gov/2024008717

FIRST EDITION

Front cover image: Doré, Gustave, 1832-1907, "Me miserable! Which way shall I fly,
Infinite wrath, and infinite despair?," reproduction of wood engraving, 1866. Image
courtesy of the Rare & Special Books Collection, University at Buffalo, The State
University of New York.
Author photo by Jacob May

Cover design by Cody Gates, Happenstance Type-O-Rama
Interior design by Maureen Forys, Happenstance Type-O-Rama

Printed and bound in the United States of America
First Edition Copyright: 2024

TRP: The University Press of SHSU
Huntsville, Texas 77341
texasreviewpress.org

## The TRP Southern Poetry Breakthrough Series
Series Editor: J. Bruce Fuller

*The TRP Southern Poetry Breakthrough Series highlights a debut full-length collection by emerging authors from each state in the southern United States.*

BOOKS IN THIS SERIES:

Alabama: Raye Hendrix, *What Good is Heaven*

South Carolina: Dan Leach, *Stray Latitudes*

West Virginia: Kelly McQuain, *Scrape the Velvet from Your Antlers*

Arkansas: James Dunlap, *Heaven's Burning Porch*

Florida: Caridad Moro-Gronlier, *Tortillera*

Georgia: Erin Ganaway, *The Waiting Girl*

Texas: Lindsay Illich, *Rile & Heave*

Louisiana: Chris Hannan, *Alluvial Cities*

Mississippi: Noel Polk, *Walking Safari: Or, The Hippo Highway*

North Carolina: Sally Stewart Mohney, *Low Country, High Water*

Tennessee: William Kelley Woolfitt, *Beauty Strip*

*for my kinfolk*

—

*for the Southern queers*

—

*for the places we love that don't love us back*

# CONTENTS

## I

## II

# III

# IV

I

# MORNING SONG

*after Brigit Pegeen Kelly*


listen: the rooster crows
        his throaty grief to the sunrise

wakes the valley
        with his undulating dirge

today the farmer takes
        the eldest of the rooster's

wives for the hen-culling
        her age a plague of need

no use wasting good seed
        on the eggless      no use feeding

the crone with her cavernous
        womb      her living hunger

inconvenient
        the farmer bears her

to her guillotine
        a nail-pronged stump

behind the coop      the nails
        hold her head in place

while the farmer holds
          her body still            pulls to stretch

her feathered neck long
          and clean for the slicing          soon

her keening populates
          the dawn          banshee-shrieks

so spectral even the cicadas
          hush their humming          even

the coyotes cease to sorrow
          their howls          then

the punctuating thump
          of hatchet          then

the sudden gurgled
          stop          then

silence          bone-white
          silence          the whole valley

chokes          on this silence
          all except the barn cat

who has been watching
          the old hen wane in secret

been waiting weeks
          for the farmer to find

2

her dreary nest          no
          the cat does not suffer

this silence          he hurries to beat
          the ants and horseflies

to the slaughter          creeps from hiding
          to gnaw the lonesome head

listen closely:
          in this silence

you can almost hear
               his patient teeth

# SINK

Pine Mountain swells above the lake
and they name it Emerald, though

in autumn I call it sunset, fire, the throats
of a thousand robins wheeling their color

to the water's sparkling dark. What lives
in the mountain's shadow becomes

part of the mountain, pools in the valley
like a child hidden in a womb not yet full

enough to see. They name the water
Emerald and when it grows they dam it,

section it in two and call the new lake Jade.
I call it robin's throat, hawk feather, clay.

The land here is low and I am lower.
Old men on mowers move through the valley

like migrating beasts, reducing everything.
I want my body to be small again

and smooth as the green-algaed stones
in mountain shadow at the bottom

of the lake. That deep, even common things
are lovely—the water's surface sifting sunlight

into autumn: a new robinfire sky; the algaed
rocks green heavy gemstones I gather in my arms.

# THE HORSE

The year before my mother
was a mother she cradled

a foal, weeks old and already
broken by desire: mimicking

its own strong mother, tried
to clear the fence and couldn't,

legs too twiggy to make the leap.
My mother watched as it crumpled

on the other side, wanted to rise
and couldn't, back bending

in ways it shouldn't, severed
spine, wrong-angled knees.

My father held the foal's real mother
by her reins while my mother

held the foal, soothed fingers
through its mane, the black head

large and heavy in her lap.
My father pulled the mare

back to the barn, called the vet
who made the dirt-road drive

at once, brought the syringe.
Later, years after my mother

had finally become my mother,
she would tell me how it felt

to hold power as it was emptied,
how she soon stopped grieving

for the horse-child to love
one of her own.

It never snows in Alabama
but my mother said

when I was born the world was hard
and white: a blizzard knocked out

the heat and while she nursed
my father blanketed the horses

that remained. I arrived to the sound
of hoofbeats, the rhythmic thump

of my father chopping down
the fence for a fire.

# THERE WERE DAISIES

I am born again every day.
Sometimes loud and rough
as righteous thunder;

sometimes cold and quiet
as a stone. It wasn't always so.
The first time I was reborn

I told my mother I wanted
to love a woman, and in answer
she told me about the rape—

so young when it happened
she and my father hoped
I wouldn't remember.

(There were daisies, I think,
on the table. The carpet smelled
of dryer sheets and clove.)

# URUSHIOL

*for Dad*


As a child I filled my hands
with what I thought were weeds
from my father's garden.

Ungloved I pulled twists
of strangling leaves from throats
of okra, unwound them
from tomato stalks to let the red
fruits gasp and heave.

Then I filled my hands
with my father, pulled him
by his wrists to my conquest
of stinging green.

We didn't make it far before the itch
began—his dark arms pink-puffed
and angry from my touch.

These are his traits I am not heir to:
      black hair
      olive skin
      arms capable of cradling a child
and, we learned that day,
      the poison of those weeds,
      *urushiol* the only fault
      I managed to escape.

(My father held me anyway.)

That night he bathed himself
in calamine, and with its pink
sheen of softness his body
almost looked like mine.

# FISHING ON SUNDAYS

When my grandfather tells me
the lake I grew up on isn't

natural, that it was dug out
of the mountainside by the sons

and grandsons of old men
who wanted a place to retire,

a place to die, I wonder if my own
father would have been

one of them—if I could have
done it: dig a lesser Heaven

for the not-yet-dead.
The next day in church

I squirm like a sinner
while nursing-home voices

sing from paper-thin hymnals
*O brothers, let's go down*

*down to the river to pray.*
I wonder if the sons

and grandsons of old men
made that river too

and if they did, why
we don't sing hymns to them

instead of God. After the service
my grandfather shakes

the preacher's hand, asks
if it's alright to fish on Sundays

as long as he throws them back.
Says he wants to show me how

to cast a line. Says it's time
I learn to bait a hook.

As he drives us home I am thinking
about hymnals and fishing line

and lures; who or what we pray to—
what we ask for—at the shore.

# NO ANGELS HERE

The rain comes relentless
to the valley to coax

the lake from its limits,
set loose all that suffers

soil. No angels here.
Not like the rapture

this unearthing:
in red floodwaters

caskets nose
the graveyard fence

like patient old canoes.
Who knew the dead

could float?
The night is so dark

it swallows everything
that moves. Even daylight

is thick and gray
with drowning. The bones

of houses buckle
and warp with wet,

sides distending, round
as the red bellies

of buoys the fishing boats
have left behind.

# WHAT THE WATER LEFT BEHIND

We didn't know that it had swallowed
Biloxi whole, or that the waves
betrayed the boats in Mobile Bay.

We didn't know the French names
of the tiny coastal towns, or that the gulf
was busy burying them in brine.

We didn't know the trawling prawners
in the shallows of Bayou La Batre gave up,
cast their lines for Heaven in the water's wake.

We didn't know we wouldn't eat shrimp
for nearly a year. In Alabama it was dark
for days. The water swept up power lines

and gas tanks, all the magnolias my father
planted the year before, their roots upturned,
outstretched like empty hands of need.

We scoured the house for batteries
for flashlights. Used none for the radio
and the news. When the light finally returned

the TV came back with it, drowning
out the overcast gloom. We should have,
but didn't know we'd see the bodies

on the news: face down, swollen, buoyant
in all the wrong ways, clogging the canal-streets
of New Orleans; or the new coastline, framed

by the screen—a perverted gift shop snapshot:
wrought-iron coral, rooftops islands, brown bay—
a postcard from a large and lonely God.

# SURFACING

*for Meemaw and Pawpaw*

We go out on the water
early morning, long before

the sun has the chance
to rub the fog from its eyes,

and we join the mist's soft
silence, dare not rouse the day

before its time. The fish,
my grandfather says, bite better

at this hour, come closer
to the shallows, lulled

to safe surfacing
by the stillness of prior night,

the slow creeping of black
to the gray light of summer

-warmed dawn. We cast
our lines, wait for the ripples

from our lures to fold back
into the whole, and soon

slick bodies slice the murk
with silvered greens

and blues, almost invisible.
A line grows taut; they scatter.

We reel one in. A bream,
my grandfather says.

A bluegill too small to eat,
too many bones.

He throws it back. I sacrifice
another worm to a hook.

We claim three fish before
the sun becomes unbearable,

only two of them worth
keeping; catch one more

before we call it quits,
feeling our skin cry out

for shade because here
the heat is thick and wet

by nine. We haul a bucket
of frantic fish to shore—bluegill

and two yellow-spotted bass—
where my grandmother waits

with a knife to relieve them
of their heads, their scales

and fins. She dispatches them
quickly, throws the useless

parts aside for the cat
who already lurks nearby.

She scrapes away
their iridescence, coats her hands

with flakes of rainbow,
makes suncatchers in the grass.

She tells me to look
at one of the lonely heads:

the way the mouth still opens
and shuts even in the absence

of a body; watch how the gills,
blue and bleeding, flex

like lungs—a different kind
of drowning. The body

in her hand moves too—
lashes out, slices her palm

with its last remaining fin,
but she is graceful; doesn't

swear. Says it's natural
to rage against the end.

# ANY COYOTE

Like tongues of fire on the mountain
the red tails of fox squirrels flicker

as they run from our presence—
the crunch of my boots, chaotic joy

of my large yellow dog who follows
them like smoke. This morning

my father sent me out with a rifle.
We're meant to be searching

for something but I can't remember
what. The woods are like that. Dark

spokes of evergreen wheel overhead
to obscure all that lives beneath

and above—their needles sew away
the sky. Behind us an owl

questions everything, and in the clear
cold air the boulders—without

their spring muffle of moss—repeat
the inquiry. Today even the wind

won't whisper its guesses through
the bare branches of trees less fortunate

than pine. The long ghost of its body
quick and gray, a coyote wisps

through the brush. My dog
pursues it out of sight, returns

with one of our missing chickens hanging
broken from his jaw. Yes, that's right:

my father sent us after the coyote—
my dog to find and I to shoot it—

while he repairs the plundered coop.
*The* coyote, he said. By which he means:

*any* coyote. My dog leads me back
to the coyote's den: a hole full of red

feathers, gnawed bone, the old blue collar
of someone's missing cat. No—I mean

*anyone's* cat. The mountain
doesn't know any of our names.

# BLOOD IN THE MILK

The calf slipped from her body
like a receding wave: breathless,

limp, landed soft and heavy
in the dew-wet grass the way

a stone might after rolling slowly
down a hill, a nine-month anti-climax—

and if cows can mourn its mother did.
Wouldn't let us close enough to milk

for days, pink udder distending,
swelling as if in place of empty womb.

She wasn't mine—belonged to the old
farmer who lived a mile around the bend,

nestled in our shared bosom of hills—
but I loved her as if she was,

and the farmer let me, gave me a key
to his barn, let my girlhood smell

of shit and seed and hay.
I walked there every day, freckles

blooming like cow-spots on my cheeks
in the early heat of April, and maybe

that's why she finally let me close:
my body not much larger than

her would-be calf's, arms and legs
twiggy, pigtails like low red ears,

my breed a mother's aggrieved
mistake for bovine. The farmer gave me

a milking stool and bucket, showed me how
to work my hands, slow as springtime,

gentle as a suckling mouth. I pulled
and when I did she looked me in the eye.

# ANIMAL INSTINCT

Walking with my dog and father through
the woods when animal detected animal,

slightest rustling in the forest floor, an infant
squirrel's squeaks sharp as a dog whistle,

pitched almost too high for human ears.
Fallen from its piney drey, eyes still sealed

with birth—I jerked the leash of my dog
to keep the creature from his maw.

My father said to leave it to die quickly—
let the dog have his merciful doggy way.

I didn't. Made a leaf into a litter and
bore the squirrel home in my palm

where it died a long slow death over days
in the rust of a long-dead hamster's cage.

How to understand that even care can be
misplaced, excessed, can make of you

a monster. How to know when kindness
means *crush* instead of *heal.*

# THE BATS

we find them in the icicle-toothed
        maw of a cracked open boulder

in the woods behind our home
        soft bodies hanging close

as cloistered nuns        tucked habit
        of dark wing        stone-shadow veil

my father says their mother
        must have loved in the wrong

season        her babies born
        in the wrong turn of the year

he says it's a wonder
        they haven't yet starved

but soon they will        no food
        to be found in winter        no insect

-hum choir for them to quiet
        in the cold        my father says

they're so still they might
        be dead already        upside down

memorials in a stonefrost church
        that night I freeze myself as well

with opened window watch
      for black wing against black sky

listen for shadow-soft sounds
      of flight      petition the stars

their heat that one might
      become a saving sun      but morning

comes in silence      the winter
      sunlight harsh and cold as moonless

night      when my father wakes
      we go to check them      find

their bodies icebound to the rock
      wings fallen      hanging stiff

above their heads like lifted
      hands in praise      or the prostrate

arms of sinners before god
      I go to move them but my father

says to leave them for the wildcats
      and the dogs that run the mountain

he asks me to be more like
      winter      beautiful but hard

he says despite my softness
            everything must eat

# MERCY

learned young in the dead
of Appalachian winter
hard air        harder soil

the raccoon curled
at the base of the drive
so still we believed

it a stone        so still
its body had time
to give in to the frost

slate fur prickling
like snow-tipped pine
mouth white with sick foam

my father        loaded gun
aimed at the neck
called this mercy

a word I'd only heard
in church sermons
spilled like coal

from the hard mouths
of preachers        only
knew as need

my father didn't shoot
gave me the rifle
said it was time I learned

mercy      this mercy
a quick trigger-pull
a bullet-split spine

this mercy      warm
blood in the palm
of barely-sticking snow

# SKINNING THE FOX

Still dark out when my father pulls
the trigger. The air rings like a bell
after the gunshot as if purified
by sound.

*Only Enoch and Elijah*
*got to leave this world alive,*
he tells me, hours later, large
hands shaving skin from pink
meat—the fox, its body strung
between us, rope cinched
around a slender foot.

The body sways as he slices,
an inconsistent pendulum
marking time it will not see;
it wiggles—almost playful, almost
dancing—skin turned down
like the skirts of girls
on playgrounds after church.

He says, *Please understand*
*I had to shoot it.* And I do.
The fox was wreaking havoc
in the hen house, the goat pen,
stealing chickens and killing kids.
My father tried to be humane.
Set traps, built better fences—
he tried. And each dawn
mocked his efforts
with the awful fuss of death.

I help him stretch the pelt
across the rack, ribbon guts
into a bucket, scrub stray blood
from the floor. He tried. *I know,*
I say. *But did we have to skin it?*
*No*, he tells me. *No,*
*That's not the point.*

II

# SQUASH GARDEN

No horses in the barn. No high-backed animals with hooves. My father worked the earth in the lake-flat valley basin, turned blood-clay into rows. His shoulders were the plow—sun-dark and toiling. He dug up rows of mountains. He might have been God. He scattered a prayer of seeds and perspired for them like rain. The heat followed him across the new country. It pulled rain from his shoulders and where it fell grew many yellow gourds, suns meant to crush between my father's daughter's teeth. My father's body plowed no sons. He grew a daughter who couldn't eat the light.

# BLOOD FOR EGGS

When it comes time to slaughter
the hogs it's the men

who do the slicing but
the women who make use

of the remains—know how
to clean and cook the skin

and muscle—substitute
the blood for eggs.

The men won't eat the dark
concoctions but their Scottish

wives who settled this valley
and their daughters

have no issue—which
they say is because women

like Christ are used
to sacrifice and stains.

When I ask my mother
how she learned to live

with all that iron she tells me
again of the womb

and crucifixion—the duty
and the nails. She says

the only women who
should be afraid of bleeding

are the ones not washed
in the blood of the Lamb.

# BARGAINING THE HURT

When I was a child one of my teeth wasn't yet loose
but it ached so badly I wanted it gone, so I bartered
the quick intensity of the pull for the long haul
of waiting out hurt: stole a bobbin from my mother's
sewing kit and looped thread around tooth
and bathroom doorknob the way I'd seen
kids do it on TV, slammed it as hard as I could—
but the door didn't catch, tugged the tooth,
then bounced back from the frame and hit me
hard in the face, drew blood from my nose
instead of mouth, the way my grandmother had
two weeks before in that same bathroom
when she pushed my head through the drywall
for being *a little dyke*, but nobody believed me,
and *how does a ten-year-old know that word, anyway?*
Again and again I rammed shut the door—what humor
is the mixture of drool and snot and tears?—
until the aching tooth was loose, thread
cutting the pink from my gums, and finally, the wet
sound of tearing, the tooth and its long root
leaving my skull in an exhale of red. Not yet covered
over, I hid the bloody thread and bobbin in the hole
my head had made. I placed the tooth under
my pillow. I got my reward. I have always been good
at knowing which secrets to keep.

# SERMON

Before the stroke he wasn't cruel,
just quiet: my grandfather a dated

Southern stoic, people thought him
cold—and after he's the same, or almost—

sometimes the wrinkles rearrange
his face into a smile, sometimes he tries

to tell me about God, how our souls
will know each other in the after.

He wants to make certain I understand
there is an *after* worth behaving for,

because he hasn't said as much, but I know
he has always suspected I don't believe.

*When we ain't in the truck the radio*
*keeps on playing somewhere else,*

he tells me, doing his best
to explain Heaven.

# GO TO CHURCH OR THE DEVIL WILL GET YOU

*after the road sign on I-65 in Chilton County, AL*

*"And when they have seen the destruction of their beloved ones, bind them fast in the valleys of the earth, 'til the day of their judgement..."*

—*The Book of Enoch*

The one visible piece of some ancient
fallen angel, the grist mill water wheel
churns beneath the red tin gaze of a devil
no larger than a man, but hoisted twice
as high. Fed by the Alabama or
an underground river's secret pulse,
the angel casts its gaze over the interstate,
keeping tabs on travelers, the silent final
witness to the people who become
white crosses on the shoulder, the people
who make people into crosses
on the shoulder, the angel's many eyes
watching everything, doing nothing,
standing useless between the devil
and those he hopes to take.

# HUSK HYMN

in the early heat
  of Bible Belt spring
    the cicadas surface

    from their hungry
  root sleep and leave
their brittle ghosts

to the trees  oak
  and pine bark hung
    with nymph skins split

    down the spine
  like strange
yolkless eggs

at first I fear them
  these husks a testament
    to growth   mirror

    of my young
  expanding chest
slow-growing

and round-soft
      as the mountains
            of my home

            at first I pull
      the mocking bodies
from the bark

and crush them
      in the bathroom mirror
            try to press my breasts

            back into sternum
      but like God's mercies
they're new every

morning and like
      God's mercies I try
            to trade them for my wants

            for months and months
      I crush them     long
beyond the sun-slick

days of April
      and the devil's hot
            lungful of July

            I grind them underfoot
      all summer     tie down
my growth

with layered lengths
        of rope but by October
                I'm a convert of necessity

                the southern heat extending
        summer and its ghosts
who follow

me close as shadows
        through home's hallways
                and the man-tall stalks

                of okra in the fields
        even to church
where I'm forced

to face the opalescence
        of my former body
                give in to my overgrowth

                of shell and sing
        with the Sunday
morning choir *praise be*

*to the cicadas who shudder*
        *off their youth*
                *unflinching*          *crack*

                *bold open the certain*
        *evidence of change*

# PRUNING

When I was young anger
bloomed in my chest
like sharp red flowers

but I wanted the garden
of my body to be shallow.
I wanted to be measured

in control.
I began collecting sharp
things from my father.

I kept them close at hand.
when the flowers opened
I was ready with the shears.

# DAUGHTER

*"The Lord disciplines those he loves, as a father the son he delights in."*

—*Proverbs 3:12*

I was loved with a Bible
        a belt    I ate Ivory

soap      I was sent out
        to choose the switch

from one of many dogwoods
        in the yard          cut

the slender branchling
        flexible enough

to sting          (the center
        still green)

when I'd done wrong
        when I was wrong

when my body      its want
        was wrong      Hate

the sin      love the sinner
        my father said

He once told me          (made me
        swear to keep it secret

to never tell my sister)
        that he loved me the most

# BAD FRUIT

The peaches turned
before I could pick them.
I told them, *Fuzzy stars,*
*I envy you*, flesh safe
from my father's teeth.

I left the grove
with all the harvest
baskets empty, kept only
for myself a single
bruising peach.

I held it close to me
for days, brought it to bed
with me each evening,
pressed it to my chest,
shared my warmth until
it felt like another body—
one I thought I could love
without consuming—

No—It wasn't my father's
teeth that needed fearing.
I ate that rotten fruit
and it was sweet.

# BOTTOMFEEDER

in church I was told I was only
good for sinking      so as a child
I skipped Sunday school      brought
a girl from class down with me
and we slicked our small bodies
through the vent in the door
to the empty daycare      sucked
sweetmilk bottles meant for babies
since we still were babies too
the butterfly of our hips had not
yet opened      with short hair
we still looked like little boys
in the first sex dream I remember
I was alone      a penis hung useless
between my adolescent legs
unwieldy      gray and hungry
as a catfish      I had to feed myself
and when I woke I knew I belonged
at the bottom of some murky depth
needed a wider mouth      I still
don't know whose body I belong to
mine or the ones who've been
inside it      or the ones I've been
inside      desire like this should be
too slippery a thing to have fins
as sharp as these      if you hold me
by my softer parts I'll still try to slice
open your palm      even when
you love me right      I thrash

# LET NOT A WOMAN

After I'm caught with my fingers
beneath her shirt at church skipping
Sunday School I am sent to a Christ

-based therapist with a self-proclaimed
77% dyke rehab success rate
and at our first session he doesn't laugh

when I say *I think that's sexual harassment*
after he asks if I've ever been touched
by the Lord.

He says I have sinned of the flesh
and I tell him I didn't fuck her. He says
I need to let him in (the Lord)

and when I say *not without permission*
I'm asked if I think the fate
of my immortal soul is funny.

*No* I say *but neither is consent.*
He tells me about conversion and says
I need to let him in (          )

because his method is most successful
when his clients comply though acquiescence
isn't required. *Let not a woman speak* he says

*Let a woman learn with silence and submission*
and when I say *No* he locks the door.
*Let not a woman speak.*

Years later I did fuck that girl
from Sunday School. But only
because she asked me. She asked

and I was good. I loved the Lord
my God my God oh my God
and so did she. And I was good.

       I was good. She told me.

# ODE TO THE GIRL FROM SUNDAY SCHOOL

It was dangerous there, but I loved you

      so completely that every streetlight

in the parking lot that night for once

      was not a searchlight but a blinking

golden moon, casting hooks of yellow

      light that pulled my fingers through

the darkness of your hair.

      All of Birmingham wet with a summer

storm, the air sticky with steam, mist

      and heat rising from the pavement

like wayward clouds returning home.

      Your hair stuck to your cheek,

your mouth—the fruity lip gloss I didn't

      like but loved to kiss away—

my eyelashes when you bent into me—

      in public, for once, unafraid, or rather

still frightened, but fear, for once, not

      as desperate in the body as desire—

still young enough that danger

      was exciting, every lamplit touch

a footfall in a minefield—the thrill

      as much the love as the not knowing

when, not if, a kiss would make it blow.

# LETTER NEVER SENT TO A ONCE-LOVER ON THE COAST

It's okay if you don't remember how it ended.
        Neither do I. For instance, I couldn't tell you

how, in February, I drove four hours south for Mardi Gras
        to meet you at the Mobile Mystics ball, or how

we stayed with your boyfriend and we both wore blue:
        you, rustling cobalt, draped in silk, and I, thirty dollars

on the sale rack from the mall, faded navy and ill
        -fitting, probably too low-cut. I stole cheap plastic

gemstones from backstage at a drag show
        from queens I considered friends and bedazzled

the neckline myself. Badly. At the ball they kept falling off
        on the dance floor, leaving wide blue holes

in my chest. I don't remember how
        we went out to the veranda to watch the boats

shiver in the harbor of the ink-black bay
        while your boyfriend went to get us drinks, or

how you reached your hand into a hole and squeezed,
        or that you called me *beautiful*, and it was cold.

I'd forgotten that when your boyfriend came back
        and asked you to dance, I poured myself out

into strangers, filled myself back up with other lonely
        strangers' hands, drank too much and took

my dress off in the bathroom. Sent you a picture
        of the cheap gold garter advertising *Carnivale*

on my thigh. I said, *come help me earn my beads*.
        You never came. By the time we left

nearly all of my gemstones were gone and I was
        open, without shine.

That night I slept alone beside a trash can full of vomit
        and listened through the wall as your body

became a home for a name that wasn't mine.
        So what. So you didn't want to marry me.

I don't even remember where we were when you told me.
        For example, I couldn't tell you it was

three months before the ball, November in Bayou La Batre,
        while we walked through the pecan grove,

cracking the clean blue air with ungathered shells
        beneath our boots, and you weren't

holding my hand when you told me about a boy
        who'd asked you to be his girlfriend

and you'd said yes, who'd asked you to the Mystics Ball
        and you agreed, but that he had an extra ticket

and you wanted me to come. As friends, you said.
        Then I drove four hours back to Birmingham alone.

So what if I don't remember how before that, in bed
        with you in August, you told me to go down

on you, then asked me to come with you
        to Dauphin Island to meet your family

for Mobile Bay Jubilee. As friends, you said, but
        you hoped that maybe knowing me might help

your parents warm up to our truth. So I came.
        Your mother was kind. Your father called me

*charming* and said if you were more like me,
        you'd find a man.

Your brother, seventeen and soaked in hormones,
        was the one who found us out.

Your father owned a catamaran and crab traps, and
        when he took us sailing to collect them

your bikini-watching brother saw us risk a kiss
        behind the sail. We begged him not to tell

and he agreed, but only if we swore to buy him booze
        'til he turned twenty-one. I shook his hand,

which made you smile. Sea the color of sky,
        sky streaked white with laughing gulls in lieu

of clouds, blue breeze of salt—
        how could we be afraid?

The traps we gathered were a panic of shellfish,
        filled with snapping shrimp and softshell crab.

Back at the house your parents boiled them
        on the porch while we lay nearby on towels.

Your skin glowed golden while I burned.
        That night your mother invited over friends

from church. They had a son our age, or maybe
        older—decent job, hair red like mine, and

unattached. At dinner he asked for your number
        and you recited it above the table

while you touched my hand below. I was staying
        in the guestroom but when the island was asleep

we snuck to shore with a blanket.
        So what if I don't remember the way

you reassured me about the boy, that you wouldn't answer
        if he called, you were just being polite.

So what if I don't remember how we hushed ourselves
       between tall walls of whispering sea oats, lay

together in the sand, our sex so quiet the sound of the ocean
       spilled from your throat instead of my name.

# HUNGER

what I know of love
is forbidden

dark sweet plum fruit
plump stars purpling

the only tree in the yard
my father says I'm not

to eat from because rot
has taken the bark

and he fears it may
have spoiled the fruit

but the branches are inviting
slung tempting low

with heavy plums
sweetness within reach

I succumb anyway
break plum from branch

and delight at the weight
in my palm the breast

heavy curve then the pop
sound of teeth breaking

human-soft skin
forbidden plum blood

slick sour evidence
wine-dark on my tongue

III

# CATALOG OF ACCEPTABLE VIOLENCE

*for Nicholas Hawkins, a bisexual teenager murdered on*
*Feb. 13, 2016, in Walker County, AL, where violence against*
*the LGBTQIA+ community is not considered a hate crime.*


a fishhook through the thumb
your grandfather removes
with pliers rusty
from rain

transubstantiation of wine
on sunday mornings—
the sons of god breaking
flesh to bread

the neighbor boys
firing pellet guns
at feral cats
behind the barn

        / /

a boy in the bed
of a truck with a shotgun
bleach and blankets

a boy left in a field
of moonlight
the consequence of kissing
other boys

*//*

a string looped around
a loose tooth
and the knob of a door
your father slams
to pull it from your skull

a bullet to the brain
of a rabid opossum
in the yard that threatens
the family dog

the boys at the rodeo
bucked by bulls
with blunted horns—
their trophies in the bruises
and the blood

# FRIDAY NIGHT LIGHTS

Day disappears behind the ridge.
The golden hour is full of smoke

from tailgates, stolen cigarettes, fathers
lighting charcoal grills in the parking lot

behind the school. Their sons—long
boys with longer shadows—march

from locker room to field,
cleats crunching the gravel path

like discordant drums of war, child
soldiers swallowed by shoulder pads,

chewing mouthguards like tobacco,
slurring words they're too young to use

at cheerleaders too young to know why
it makes them tug at the hems

of their skirts, use their pom-poms
to shield their adolescent thighs.

They are learning to be women
from the boys who are learning

to be men by learning how to take a hit
or hit harder than their fathers.

The whistle blows; bodies collide.
The whole town begins to scream.

# PREY

When the sun could no longer
warm me I swallowed a goldfinch.

Rain brought bluebirds
and I stood in the watermelon field,

my mouth holding seeds.
The bluebirds clotted

in my throat like clouds
but their color did not create in me

a sky. Instead their softness
made them prey: my body a walled

place to hunt, birds in a barrel
waiting to be caught—my body

a roost for osprey, turkey vulture,
hawk. They sank their talons low

in my belly, consumed every lark
and sparrow I coaxed beyond

my teeth. I should have extended
mercy to the songbirds:

scarecrowed my arms wide
and frightening, sealed my lips

with thread, but each day I stood
in the field, mouth open, a nest.

# DOVES IN THE IVY

Three white-winged doves
nest in the poison ivy patch

my father has been asking
me to cut down for weeks

since—despite my body's
other failings—I have not

inherited the itch.
I could lie down with them—

the doves—so safe they must
be women. Which is unfair.

My father is gentle, and was
raised by another gentle man—

though I have seen them both
go wild with rage in ways

my mother never has.
My father is a gentle man:

he gave me my first
shotgun, taught me how

to shoot—to kill quickly,
show mercy—and only

when I must. The last time
he hunted for sport, before

I was a thought, he shot
a squirrel, which his mother

stuffed and mounted
in her house where it stayed,

collecting dust, until the day
she died because my father

wouldn't have it in his home,
couldn't look the creature

in its imitation eyes,
his guilt unbecoming

of a southern man.
I wanted to be a southern

man. To love a southern
woman. Feel guilt for nothing.

# THE EPITHETS OF LOCAL SHELLS

That was the night my mother burned
my father's birthday dinner.
But let me start again.

My mother's hands were small,
barely large enough to hold.
But she could hold shells, so that night

I brought her what I'd found in the river,
the hard skins of mussels. I gave them
reverently as treasure, the empty husks

opening like lungs or cartoon hearts
in the soft bowl of her palm, crude
calcium butterflies beautiful only

to me and her. She taught me their names.
*These pale ones are Pink Mucket. These*
*are Pigtoes. The black ones are called Heelsplitters.*

*They're the ones your father hates.*
While dinner cooked she pooled
me in her lap. That was the year my father

worked late every night but not
because he wanted to. That was the year
there were layoffs and he needed to prove

his worth, because we didn't have much money
and my mother couldn't find a job.
But that's not what she told me.

That year my father's birthday fell in the middle
of the week, and he didn't make it home
in time to eat. My mother touched a mussel,

shell worn to iridescence. She told me,
*This one is my favorite, Painted Creekshell.*
And the kitchen began to slowly fill with smoke.

# OMEN

The whip-poor-will speaks a tongue I understand:
warm humid evenings, pine petrichor and litterfall,
the Cahaba lily's beautiful day-long life, a perfect
metaphor for grief.

Local legend says to hear one wakes a death,
sends it to your doorstep like an unwanted
salesman in a crisp gray suit.

Once, atop Pine Mountain with my father
a whip-poor-will sang as he showed me a large
slope of limestone, coal and iron ore
ribboning its ancient face.

His rough hand swept the air like a composer
as he traced the subtle dark waves in the stone,
keeping time with the one-two-three
waltz of the dusk bird's call, until—

was it coincidence or omen—the ambulance wail,
the bird's sudden flight that turned our eyes
away and east, toward home, a beacon
in the quickening night.

We descended to find our family, whole.
We ate supper in silence, listened to someone's
sad animal sounds echo across the valley,
the whip-poor-will singing—this time—not for us.

# FIRE ON THE MOUNTAIN

Barefoot on the front lawn, three AM—
the grass should have been green and wet

with dew. Across the street, the useless lake
shriveled to shallows like a pool of slick

black oil in the night, waiting to burn.
Behind us, the mountain, the fire

on the mountain sweeping through
the dry pines, smoke rolling like fog,

crackle and roar obscuring August
crickets, bullfrogs, yipping coyotes calling

their young. Our house backlit in red.
We hold our breath, or try to—wait

for the hum of fire helicopters sent from the city,
hovering low with their heavy, big-bellied loads.

Suddenly, a sound: an awful warbling keen;
suddenly, a vision: the forest opens

like a Hell-mouth, hot and black, spits out
a frantic, lonely doe, her body alight, a comet

splitting the night as she burns toward the lake—
the water that should save her, but won't.

# BLUE RIDGE LOOKOUT

Days after the forest fires
and the air is still thick enough

to smudge the fogged ridges
with a finger, wipe away

the smoke to reveal rows
of secret mountains, valleys,

hidden flocks of birds born
as if already in flight, windstruck

to the canvas of the sky.
In the hollers forgotten stills

gleam like the last gold teeth
in a mouth when the haze

opens for a slip of sun, copper
monuments to moonshine,

bootleggers long gone.
And this abandoned lookout

station wasted by the fires,
its bones scaffolding what's left

of the scorched black mountainside,
concrete and iron the only things

the heat couldn't consume, a frame.
This is how it goes: we burn

the mountains and die
in a world without mountains.

We don't have any clue
how to make a bird.

# RIPENING

That year, the first tomato
to ripen was useless at its peak:
deceptively red, life-swollen,

but within it, nothing—save
a bloody, worm-eaten pulp.
All summer I stayed in the sun

checking still-green tomatoes
for worms until my skin was close
to the hue I hoped they'd grow into,

until my hands, deep in the thick
of leaves, became fruits
on the vine, waiting to be worthy

of use. I learned to photosynthesize.
Learned to love the birdsong
and the rain, forgot I was not

a tomato, that I was able to let go—
didn't have to wait for rot
or bug-hunger to take me first—and still

I clung to the stalk like a white-
knuckled lover, more fearful of releasing
than the distance to the ground.

# DROUGHT

Summer held thunder
to the mountainside
like a lover but offered

nothing—heat lightning
the false prophet of rain—
a chalk-dry sky that swallowed

the moon and everything blue.
My mother didn't believe
in omens but that year

I caught her lighting candles
for want of water, found
my father staring

at what was left of the lake—
the way its cracked shoreline
curled like the mocking smile

of a skull.
On Sunday mornings
the preacher said it was sin—

our secret pleasures—
that kept the rain at bay
so men lined up all summer

to be baptized and all
the women started wearing
white.

The week after the abortion
I wanted to be heavy
so despite the drought

I swallowed water in secret,
wrapped my body around
whatever spigot I could find

while the pious prayed
for rain, and like Judas
kissing cheeks on Sundays

I prayed with them—tested
the weight of water on my knees—
but when it finally came

it flooded everything.
Uprooted anything
that might have grown.

# DESIGN FLAW

The crickets play their wing song
to an audience of dark.
Cicadas rattle tymbals in the sun.
White tails of deer blink
through the forest shade, signaling
retreat while the bobcat creeps
behind on certain, silent feet.
Every body in this valley working
as it's meant to. I don't know
what it means to be a woman
with heavy, childless breasts.
When I rub my legs with other legs
they do not make a sound.

# THE DARKEST PLACE IN ALABAMA

Milk splashed in a great black empty cauldron—
the stars—so thick they embarrass the moon,
seem to drip from the dark pail of the sky
into the river, the pines—a silver
lining to isolation, the loneliness
of too much land with too few people
in it. Godless in God's country, I count
myself their kinfolk—those distant clustered
suns, Heaven's fiery queers that seem so close
but never touch, glittering together
and alone, spread beyond the reach of love.
No blood, thick or otherwise, to speak of,
no resemblance, no relation, still I call
them family, celestial cousins,
but I am most like the stars in that I consume
myself in absence. What else is there
to do in all that empty space but burn?

# AGAINST SALVATION

if beauty is a sin give me
beauty           if gluttony
a fork and knife      let
me drink the sweet water
of youth's fountain while
young            waste it
deliciously       gulp every
brief drop         no going
back       no turning
unless it's into a pillar
of salt      if sloth
give me the luxury
of convenience and a lover
to decay with        of angels
and their offices      I want
no part      except maybe
the ones who lusted
desired more or anything
other than an eternity of peace
golden palaces with pearl
-laid streets          gold bores
me       peace bores me
I cannot eat a pearl
if I must confess and repent
to enter paradise      I confess
I don't want it            I repent
of nothing        but the time
spent fearing holy wrath      gold

pearls, saints, paradise sounds
like it would bore me          so
if Heaven is a paradise
I will face God and dance
backwards into Hell
which can't be that much
worse than Alabama
if eternal life is what I lose
for loving her          give me her
and the quick burn
of mortality          and
if mortality is a curse
o god          I beg of you
curse me          curse me
curse me          forever and ever          amen

# THE HERON

Serious as deacons, a siege
of great blue herons move

through the gray morning
mist on the water with slow,

backward-kneed precision,
their number doubling almost

perfectly in the barely-stirred glass
of the lake. The valley is silent,

glaucous, the ghost of evening
moseying through the hickory

and cattails like it's got nowhere
to be. One heron slips away,

nears the soft shore, the rusting
traps the fisherfolk laid for crawfish

and minnows, bait for bigger game.
She dips her head beneath the water,

graceful as a debutante, long
beak angling through the entry,

hunger pushing her deeper,
further, too far. The trap

too heavy for her beautiful neck
to lift, iron bars barbing her skull,

she thrashes, shrieks, her dampened
cries the cries of something ancient,

Mesozoic— lost to time, which won't
remember; to water, which won't forget—

even after, when the ripples and wide
blue wings go still, float instead of fly,

and beneath the surface a golden eye
stares, unforgiving, towards Heaven.

# BLOODLETTING

first the Egyptians, then
the Greeks: Hippocrates
believed we were made
of world and when the world
was too much in us, sick
manifested as an imbalance
of humors: an excess
of bile and blood

　　　 / /

when I was a child
I found the always-
locked shed behind
my grandfather's house
not locked

inside, a wild hog hung
upside down from the beams
and bled into a bucket
from a slice to the throat

when I asked my grandfather
why, he said once the hog
was empty
it would be clean

//

to heal the deepest
bruises, find a sharp
instrument of quick
clean steel

seek out the locus
of greatest pain and push
the blade inside

when the darkest blood
rises to the surface, know
that you are being
made well

//

when I was a child
my grandmother
had home remedies
for every ailment, learned
from her mother
and her mother's mother prior:

whiskey for a fussy infant
snow for frostbitten toes
bloody teeth to cure a queer

when I was sick she fed me
water like the hog:
upside down

*//*

if the Greeks can be believed
then opening a vein
is Hippocratic: violence
cloaked in an oath of care

if it's true, someday I will say
to my lover: *come to me*
*hungry as the leeches*
*that cling to moss-slick*
*stones in the creek bed*
*hang me by my ankles*
*in your room*

*I have been waiting*
*for you to bleed me*
*with your lovely*
*open mouth*

# HURT IN THE SOLE OF EVERY JOY

*for Mama*

My mother has told me how,
when she was young, she broke
a glass in her own mother's
kitchen, and fearful of the scold
she cleaned it up too quickly,
missed the thinnest shard, invisible
on the tile, which she found
hours later with a bare heel;

      and how, while hopping
to a chair to pull the sliver out
she lost her balance, and
with animal instinct
stopped herself from falling
with weight on the wrong foot,
burying the splinter deeper,
beyond the blood and callous
into the soft heart of flesh;

      and how she tore
her skin with tweezers trying
to dig it out, and failed; how
she forced a straight face or
a smile through pain, walked
without a limp to keep
her mother in the dark;

how, over time,
she almost forgot the glass
was even there, the reminder
most often coming on the heels
of delight: a thoughtless turn
while barefoot dancing,
the shifting weight from hip
to hip while trying on
impractical pairs of shoes;

and how, years later,
she finally told a doctor,
who found the buried sliver
on an x-ray, who said
at this point, the glass
is part of her body—said
more pain would come
from its removal
than if she let it be, so
she let it be—the potential
for pain in the pulse
of every pleasure, the shadow
of hurt in the sole of every joy.

This is the way I understand
the bravery of love.

# WHEN THERE IS NOTHING ELSE TO DO WE DRIVE

We take to the highways in summer, when
cricketsong seems to threaten oblivion,
when we question not what katydid or
katydidn't but *who really is this katy,*
*and why is she always doing?*
I cannot bear to watch another sunset
and you hate crickets, katydids, hate them
all, and anyway, we're out of limes
to sweeten up the beer. When it bites
we wander to my car. Southern heat holds us
heavy to the parched leather seats, cracking like
noiseless fireworks, sighing gray, apathetic
beneath my unimpressive thighs—but yours
are lovely. My car does not mind holding you.

# APIARY

*for Jacob*

The hive hangs above us
      like prayer in the willow,

honeycomb folding
      like waves on a small

golden pond.
      You tell me honeybees

have hearts but not
      for long, their lives

bound in one turn
      of spring & summer.

Of our own existence
      you say if fate is kind

we can expect three
      billion heartbeats

before death silences
      the sound. Lover,

I have missed so many
      of yours already, spent

so few summers
        swarming in your flowers.

Lover, let me hide
        your heart in a fist

of honeybees,
        muffle the sound

with the hum of sweet
        -making wings. If time

can't hear the beating
        maybe it'll pass you by,

like bees over water,
        sensing nothing to take.

# SOUTHERN THESAURUS

*The Devil's beating his wife*
which is to say the world
shimmers like a God
-sized fistful of finely
powdered pearls.

*Out yonder way*
by which I mean anything
beyond the distant point
past which we cannot see.

*That dog won't hunt*
is hopeless and when
the weatherman says *polygon*
it means find a bathtub,
basement, ditch, and pray.

If you *holler* in a *holler*
you might hear your echo.

*Bless your heart*
is most often not
a blessing.

Any woman
*in the family way*
(*bless her heart*)
had better have a husband.

A *.22* is what fathers use
to threaten local boys
so their daughters don't
end up unmarried women
*in the family way.*

*If the Good Lord's willing and the creek don't rise*
it'll all turn out okay.

If you ask for help you're
*soft,* but you'll get it.

If you ask for a *Coke*
we will answer, "What kind?"
and it won't have anything
to do with a drug.

*No child of mine*
means failure, or
any parent whose child
turns out liberal, or atheist
or queer, but—

*Gettin' saved* or
*a good whippin'*
can, *Good Lord willing,*
fix it all.

*Concubine,* my grandmother
called her—the unmarried woman
who lived with a man
in a double-wide down the street.

That man was a *lawyer*,
which rhymes with "flaw"
and most nearly means
the same thing: a sinner.

*Concubine,* even though
they never did have children—
a childless woman.
That was worse.

# PINSON

What will it take to stop thinking
of here as home? I stay, I go, I come

again—even the shifting skyline
seems the same, new buildings owned

by old money, old trees felled
for a different kind of growth,

the streets still keepers
of slave owners' names.

The corrupt Mayor died but now there's
another reclining in his chair.

Always more, an abundance of Mayors,
a plague. The Dairy Queen torn

down and resurrected as a failing
strip mall is still *the place*

*that used to be the Dairy Queen.*
The husk of the grocer on Old

Springville Road still wears the ghost
of its former life, *Piggly Wiggly*

shadowed into brick by years of heat
and sun. This entire miserable town—

its dilapidated roads pothole-pocked
and going nowhere—a relic of itself

inhabited by rot, the kind that sticks
around, keeps itself alive, blooms

sickly where nothing else will—
where the people are proud

to be holdout Confederates,
each new generation baptized in red.

But there's jasmine here. There's light.
The tea is cold and smooth and sweet

and brewed by a windowed sun.  Dogs
wear no collars. Cats lie fat and happy

on the warm roofs of trucks—fed full
by field mice and table scraps

from women with curlers in their hair—
unowned and belonging to us all.

The mountain breeze cools the air,
ripples the lake to diamonds, the algae

a million emeralds sunk just beyond
the shore, a jeweled city for channel cat

and bass. And the people plant
things. Put down roots. Let kudzu

stabilize disintegrating barns, hold up
the walls. Is it wrong of me to want

this to survive? To die? To leave,
come home, then leave again

and leave my ghost behind?

# ADVANCED THANATOLOGY

most days / I imagine my death
in color /or as an itchy ache

tangible as the calamus
of goosefeather needling through

the fabric of the blanket
on my bed / discomfort taking

the place of warmth / for example
the dream of my death is a study

in red / where I am young
and my mother is always there

insistent as the sunrise / and alive
by which I mean / her existence

in that dream is the reason
I have never been able

to believe / I will grow old
the most natural thing in life

I'm told / is a child will bury
her parents / not the other way

around /so it must be that I am not
as god intended / my wants unnatural

and crude / for example I didn't love
that blanket til it hurt me

and after that I couldn't sleep
without the ache / for example

I didn't know I feared my mother
until I realized / she would age

# FOX THAW

the little fox     her red body
       hard with freeze

calls to me from the roadside
       at the near edge

of spring     she asks me
       how long

it takes a body to break down
       in the cold

because she's tired
       of waiting

I admit     I'm not sure
       my own body

January-born and icy
       has been trying

to pull apart
       for years

# REVELATIONS

there is an atomic horse on the horizon      galloping

      its mane a mushroom cloud

toward my porch

(I meant to say *horseman*           but I have never

      remembered scriptures the way

they were written)

when I was a child we kept horses and my mother

      told me they were holy      said their high backs

brought us closer

to god       but never said which one

      I bet anything tall could do that      I bet

I could find a god

on top of the barn           changing the name

      of atmosphere           turning the cocksure

weathervane with its breath

but I've built myself a god already

        I call her *Night Mouth*       like me

she's always hungry

her body is made entirely of want

        she is the god-horse bursting

from its cage

to free my mother's kept horses

        and all our borrowed bales of hay

# HOME

the elusive dark : slow curve
of a mother's spine : riverbank
solid enough to stand : home
a starsilver river of arms

my mother's riverbend is subtle
& soft : her arms wet firefly
light : home the far shore of her heart
& i : the traveler boatless

//

a green fish rises from my mother's
water : shows me how to take apart
my bones : how to break & reposition
them to make of me a boat

ribcage hull : femur mast : scaffolding
of tibia & spine : if i leak i fill the gaps
with teeth : the fish says if i use my skin
for sails i won't need my mother's body

*yes* i say *but who*
*will brush my hair*

# WHAT GOOD IS HEAVEN

when my mother dreamed of children she pictured
    things in bowls        beautiful fish gracing over

brightly colored stones    clear water    a bowl of her favorite
    fruits    ceramic overflowing pears and tangerines

blueberries fat    with sweet    I have always lived in secret
    loved the dark water    I have always been

the rough-pocked bitter pit of peach    I remember being born
    or at least the second time    when as a child

I stumbled toddling    down the steep gravel road    down
    off the sharp shoulder into    a twisting bed of briar

and saw myself split    open on the thorns    witnessed
    what 'til then had only    been inside: bee balm blossoms

on my arms and knees    a secret my body well kept
    even then I tried to bury it    force self back

into antonym of self    but dying is not the same as being
    un-born    and I have never been any good at either

once it didn't rain for weeks    but I wanted to be a fish so badly
    I jumped off our pier and broke both ankles

in the drought-shallow shoals    and smiled that their new angles
    looked like fins    once I watched my father

stripping dry-rotten wood from our porch  and as he pried
        up the boards a family of opossums hissed like bulbous

vampires at the sunlight before they lit out for the edge
        of the woods      babies bobbing after mother like lures

on a troubled lake        everything is always looking
        for some new way to disappear

after the porch was fixed I loosened a board and crawled inside
        over and over      each time pretending

I was crawling to the bottom        of my mother's bowl of dream
        fruit      something soft and pitless each time

I would emerge        in the dark even the light
        -slatting planks were as large as black eternal sky

beams signaling Heaven or the break of dark
        water to surface      the sun-clear water of day

even now I am always searching for something
        to crawl into      some new way to be born

what good is Heaven to me anyway        what good
        are fish and fruit and day      I'm still the child

I always have been      hidden dark beneath the porch
        pretending every nail hole is a star

# NOTES

"Urushiol" (8) is the name of the toxin in poison ivy, poison oak, and poison sumac that most people are allergic to.

"No Angels Here" (11) and "What the Water Left Behind" (12) refer to Hurricane Katrina and its aftermath.

"Let Not a Woman" (40) references the Bible verse 1 Timothy 2:12, "But I suffer not a woman to teach, nor to usurp authority over the man, but to be in silence."

"Advanced Thanatology" (82) borrows its title from an episode of the TV show, *Supernatural*.

# PUBLICATION ACKNOWLEDGMENTS

Poems from this book have appeared in the following publications:

*Anomaly, The Boiler, Blue River Review, The Chattahoochee Review, Cimarron Review, Columbia Poetry Review, Doubleback Review, elsewhere, McNeese Review, Passages North, Poetry Birmingham Literary Review* (UK), *Poetry Northwest, Screen Door Review, Southern Indiana Review, Stained: An Anthology of Writing about Menstruation* (Querencia Press), *The Seventh Wave, The Southern Poetry Anthology Vol. X: Alabama* (Texas Review Press), *Tinderbox Poetry Journal,* and *Zone 3.*

# PERSONAL ACKNOWLEDGMENTS

None of this would be possible without the love and support of my family, blood and chosen. Thank you to all y'all who call me kin, but especially my Mama, Daddy, and sister Leslie for being so unlike the family in these poems, for being my home in this world, and for letting me use our lives for inspiration. I feel unbelievably lucky I get to call y'all mine. Thank you to Papa for your care and generosity, and to the grandparents in the great beyond for the love you gave me while you were here. Thank you to my best friend and forever first-reader, John Gulledge, who is both my tether to this planet and my release from it. Endless appreciation for my partner Jacob, for your love, support, jokes, gentleness, and for feeding me. I could not abide this life without you. And thanks to my cats, Merlin, Turnip, and Jackalope, for keeping me company while I write. I love you. Meow.

I've had the incredible fortune to have some of the kindest, most brilliant teachers. Thank you to Keetje Kuipers, who showed this shy kid from unincorporated Blount County that any of this was even possible. Thank you to my amazing Auburn University advisors Rose McLarney and Anton Disclafani. Thank you to my teachers at the University of Texas at Austin: Natalie Diaz, Jane Miller, Chad Bennet, and especially Lisa Olstein and Roger Reeves, my dream thesis committee, who saw this book taking shape in its earliest days and showed me what it could be.

All my love to the friends who played a role in the making of this book. Thank you to Auburn beloveds Richard Tyler, Carl Langlois, Kathleen Kent, Emily Enfinger, Teresa Peppers, Angela Farmer, and Emily Friedman. So much gratitude for the friends I made in Austin who saw many of these poems in their earliest days and held them gently, but especially Annelyse Gelman, Leah Yacknin-Dawson,

August Huerta, Leah Hampton, Micah Bateman, and Jessica Hincapie.

Thank you to those who read this book in earlier versions: John, Annelyse, Sebastián Páramo, and Han VanderHart. Y'all's generosity astounds me. Thank you, too, to the folks and friends who encouraged me when I felt like giving up: Rachel Combs, Anthony Garrett, Luke Johnson, Gabrielle Bates, Patrycja Humienik, C.T. Salazar, Alyssandra Tobin, Jose Hernandez Diaz, Halley Cotton, Ross White, Erin Elizabeth Smith, and so many more than I can name.

I'm so grateful to the schools and organizations that gave me funding, space, and time to write this book: Auburn University; the UT Austin's New Writers Project and Michener Center for Writers; the Bread Loaf Writers Conference; the Juniper Summer Writing Institute; and the Sundress Academy for the Arts.

Finally, thank you to everyone at TRP, but especially my editor J. Bruce Fuller, for seeing this book, for seeing me, for sharing in my complicated love of the South.

It is such a gift to be known.

# ABOUT THE AUTHOR

Raye Hendrix is the author of the chap-books *Fire Sermons* (Ghost City Press, 2021) and *Every Journal is a Plague Journal* (Bottle-cap Press, 2021). Her poems appear in *American Poetry Review, Poetry Northwest, 32 Poems, Cimarron Review*, and elsewhere. The winner of the 2019 Keene Prize for Literature and the 2018 Patricia Aakhus Award (*Southern Indiana Review*), they have also received fellowships from Bread Loaf, the Oregon Humanities Center, and the Juniper Writing Institute. Raye holds a BA and MA from Auburn University, an MFA from the University of Texas at Austin, and a PhD from the University of Oregon.